O9-BUA-129

HOMEMADE CHRISTMAS

101 Tree- TRIMMING IDEAS

Ellyn Sanna

BARBOUR
PUBLISHING

Published by Barbour Publishing, Inc., P.O. Box 719, Uhrichsville, Ohio 44683, www.barbourbooks.com

 Member of the
Evangelical Christian
Publishers Association

Printed in Italy.
5 4 3 2 1

O Tannenbaum

O Christmas tree, O Christmas tree,
How lovely are your branches.
In summer sun, in winter snow,
A dress of green you always show.
O Christmas tree, O Christmas tree,
How lovely are your branches.

*T*he evergreen tree strung with lights and colored balls often stands at the heart of our homes' Christmas decorations. When the tree is up, we know Christmas is really here.

Although the Christmas tree tradition has its roots in many pagan celebrations, it is also a truly Christian symbol, as well. In fact, Martin Luther, the great Protestant reformer, is credited with starting the custom of decorating trees for Christmas. Walking home one clear winter night, he is said to have looked up and seen stars shining through the branches of an evergreen tree. The scene was so lovely that he recreated it by bringing a tree into his home and fastening candles to its branches. "Christ's tree," he called it, a symbol of our evergreen life in Jesus—He who is the Light of the world.

Starchy String Ornaments

MATERIALS

thick cotton string
liquid starch

colored cellophane
white glue

Place string in liquid starch to soak. Arrange in desired shapes on top of colored cellophane and, using white glue, drizzle all around each shape; lay another sheet of cellophane on top and allow to dry. Cut out around the outside of the string shapes; punch holes through tops and string to hang from chandelier, in front of windows, or on the tree.

Angel Ornaments

MATERIALS

white poster paint

stiff blue paper

markers

white glue

glitter glue

clear contact paper

gold cord

Have children dip their hands in white poster paint and transfer prints to blue paper in a fan pattern. Let dry and cut out to create angel wings. Cut out an angel head (circular shape) and body (triangular shape) from additional paper, and glue wings and head to body. Children may draw details of face, hair, and angel gowns. Add glitter to a sparkly halo. Place completed angel between two sheets of clear contact paper and cut around outer edge to laminate. Punch a hole in the top and hang with gold cord.

And, lo,
the angel of the Lord came upon them,
and the glory of the Lord shone round about them. . . .
And the angel said unto them,
Fear not: for, behold,
I bring you good tidings of great joy.

LUKE 2:9–10

Angels, from the realms of glory,
Wing your flight o'er all the earth;
Ye who sang creation's story,
Now proclaim the Messiah's birth:
Come and worship. Come and worship.
Worship Christ, the newborn King!

Pom-Pom Wreaths for the Tree

MATERIALS

white glue
package of green pom-poms
wooden drapery ring
red embroidery floss (or string)

package of tiny red
pom-poms
narrow ribbon

Glue green pom-poms one by one onto drapery ring until completely covered and ring looks like a wreath. Glue a few tiny red pom-poms onto wreath for berries. Let dry. Pull a festive patterned ribbon through the hook on the ring and tie. Hang from embroidery floss pulled through the hook.

Golden Lamé Ornaments

MATERIALS

½ yard gold lamé
½ yard white
  polyester backing

cotton and metallic
  threads
small bag of polyester
  stuffing

Draw simple star and crescent moon patterns on paper, about 3 inches across. Fold fabric in half with right sides together; pin on patterns and trace outlines with a pencil. Cut through both layers adding a ¼-inch seam allowance. Baste along penciled outline leaving a 1½-inch hole for stuffing. Machine-stitch using ¼-inch seams and clip seams at angles of star arms and at ¼-inch intervals on concave curve of moon. Turn shapes right side out and fill with polyester filling. Hand-stitch opening closed and run metallic thread through tip of each ornament for hanging.

Sparkling Prisms to Light Your Tree

MATERIALS

chandelier prisms (available at home center stores)

wire ornament hangers

12-inch pieces of ribbon

Simply attach an ornament hanger to the top of the prism and tie a dainty bow (something Victorian and lacy looks nice) at the top, allowing the ribbon ends to trail down the sides of the prism. This technique can also be used to create unique ornaments using old pieces of cast-off jewelry.

Lacy Heart Tree Ornaments

MATERIALS

candy cane

2½-yard piece of 4-inch-wide ruffled lace

glue gun

small silk rose

thin piece of ribbon

Sew a casing in lace starting half an inch from plain edge. Cut lace in half and insert candy cane into each piece, gathering ruffle as you go. Attach candy canes at bottom and top with glue gun to form a heart. When dry, attach silk rose at center point with glue and affix ribbon loop at back for hanging.

*In him was life;
and the life was the light of men.
And the light shineth in darkness;
and the darkness comprehended it not. . . .
That was the true Light,
which lighteth every man
that cometh into the world.*

JOHN 1:4–5, 9

Ribbon Tree

(an alternative to an evergreen tree)

MATERIALS

5-inch Styrofoam ball
12-inch wooden dowel or
    squared wood trim, for stem
basket
ready-to-mix cement

selection of ribbons in
    different colors and
    widths, about 6 1/2 yards
    of each
florist's spool wire
reindeer moss

Spear the Styrofoam ball on the dowel. Mix enough cement to almost fill the lined basket and pour in. Place dowel in center of basket and secure with a web of masking tape across the top of pot. Let dry for 24 hours. Cut ribbon in strips 7 inches long. Double up ribbon to form single-loop bows and twist wire around center, leaving one long end to stud ball completely with bows. Spread reindeer moss out over base of tree.

Jingle Bell Tree

MATERIALS

lightweight wire
wire cutters
red berry cluster
sprigs of evergreen

large gold jingle bell
(available at craft
and fabric stores)
$1\frac{1}{4}$ yards of 2-inch-
wide sheer ribbon

Wire berry cluster and evergreen together; run wire through hanging loop of jingle bell. Thread ribbon through hanging loop and tie a bow in ribbon about 7 inches above the ornament.

Jingle bells, jingle bells,
Jingle all the way!
O what fun it is to ride
In a one-horse open sleigh!

TRADITIONAL

Mobiles for the Tree

Create a variety of mobiles for the little ones in the family using mobile wires (available at craft stores), monofilament thread, and any of the following:

MATERIALS

cutout greeting cards	tree ornaments
toy airplanes	tiny stuffed animals
angels	

Or use leftover scraps of fabric to cut out little figures or other Christmas shapes to sew and stuff—anything with bright colors and prints to stimulate baby's eyes. The important thing to remember in composing a mobile is maintaining balance. Begin hanging dangling things from top wires using thread. Adjust lengths of string to balance each side and work downward, adding new wires and hooks to keep in balance. Don't crowd objects together.

Patriotic Tree

Decorate a tree with miniature variations of the American flag reflecting different periods of our nation's history. Include any other ornaments that fit with this theme such as stars, eagles, toy soldiers, drums, etc.

Wire Treetop Star

To make this star, simply shape and twist lengths of 12-gauge and 26-gauge wire. Make the basic form with the larger wire and wind the smaller wire across the completed form for a bright and shiny treetop ornament.

When they saw the star,
they rejoiced with exceeding great joy.

MATTHEW 2:10

Star of wonder, star of night,
Star with royal beauty bright;
Westward leading, still proceeding,
Guide us to thy perfect light!

JOHN HENRY HOPKINS, JR.

Spiky Christmas Stars

Cut a circle 6 inches in diameter from silver or gold foil. Mark off 8 equal sections, being careful not to draw a line to the center of the circle. Leave a circle about $1\frac{1}{2}$ inches in diameter in the center. Cut along each of the fold lines. With the tip of a sharp pencil, start folding the edges of each cut section in a clockwise fashion. Continue rolling each section until the piece takes on the shape of a cone. Cut several more of these circles following these steps. Put one layer on top of the first so that the points of one circle fall in the open spaces of the layer below. Continue placing each layer upon layer, gluing the centers together until you have formed a half ball. The more layers you place on top of one another, the fuller the ornament will appear. Then make a second half ball and glue both halves together. Hang from the tree with transparent thread.

Ribbon Candy Ornaments

With a needle and metallic thread, run through a length of colorful ribbon at regular intervals. Draw up to create ribbon candy effect, knot, and create loop for tree hanger.

Peppermint Stick Icicles

Wrap strips of silver paper and red ribbon together around cyclinder-shaped object to create spirals. Sew silver thread through top of "candy cane" or "icicle," tie thread around artificial holiday greenery and berries, and hang it from tree.

Checkerboard Quilt Ornaments

Cut slits in paper squares and weave bits of ribbon in and out using different color combinations for quilt effect. Outline and hang "quilt" with bric-a-brac.

Snowman Tree

Have your children each make little paper snowmen to represent themselves, printing their names across the bottom, and pasting twigs on trunk for arms. Wrap with gaily colored ribbon for scarf. Paste longer twig to bottom of snowmen and anchor in a basket of pinecones to create the tree. This might be a nice gift for a family of cousins to create for grandparents with tiny school pictures cut out and pasted on the head of each snowman.

Snowball Ornament

Materials

12-gauge wire
wire cutters
plastic foam balls in assorted
  sizes
needle-nose pliers

plaster mix
old spoon
pearlescent white spray
  paint
white glitter

Cut a length of wire and insert it almost all the way through a foam ball. Using pliers, twist the wire into a curlicue or curl it around a pencil to form a spiral. Mix the plaster according to manufacturer's directions until it's the consistency of thick frosting. Dip the ball in plaster; use a spoon to spread the plaster evenly over the ball. Hang the ball to dry, suspending it on a string stretched between two chairs, spreading newspaper below to catch drips. Allow 24 hours to dry, then spray with paint, sprinkle with glitter, and dry. Attach to a bow and add clusters of berries for color.

*Purge me with hyssop,
and I shall be clean:
wash me,
and I shall be whiter than snow.*

PSALM 51:7

Come now, and let us reason together. . .
though your sins be as scarlet,
they shall be white as snow.

ISAIAH 1:18

Paradise Trees

Another source for the Christmas tree tradition can be traced back to the medieval miracle plays performed during the fourteenth and fifteenth centuries on the twenty-fourth of December. Since few people could read in medieval times, miracle plays acted out stories from the Bible. In the early church calendar of saints, December 24 was Adam and Eve's Day, so the dramatic events of the fruit tree and the Garden of Eden were depicted. Before the performance, the actors would often parade through the streets, and "Adam" would carry the "paradise tree," which was usually an evergreen tree decorated with apples. This was the only prop on stage during the play, so long after the miracle plays were no longer performed, it was connected in people's minds with Christmas.

Paradise Tree Decorations

The paradise tree was hung with apples, cherries, and white wafers or cookies. The apples symbolized the forbidden fruit and the fall of humankind, while the white wafers represented the communion bread, symbolic of humanity's salvation through Jesus Christ. Their presence on the same tree showed that even though humanity was sinful, God had provided a means to salvation. The cherries were also a symbol of hope that came from an old Christian legend. According to the story, Mary and Joseph were walking in a garden full of cherries when Mary told him about the visitation of the angel. Joseph didn't believe her, and afterward, when she asked him to pick her some cherries, he refused. Miraculously the branches of the cherry trees bent so low that Mary could reach them.

For God so loved the world,
that he gave his only begotten Son,
that whosoever believeth in him
should not perish, but have everlasting life.

JOHN 3:16

He became the author of
eternal salvation unto all them
that obey him.

HEBREWS 5:9

Modern-Day Paradise Tree

Decorate your tree with apple and cherry decorations made of wood, resin, plastic, or any other material.

WHITE WAFERS
(not edible)

MATERIALS

white bake-clay
two ⅛-inch lattice strips
white satin ribbon for hanging

cross pendant
X-acto knife
white glue

Trace pattern outline onto sturdy cardboard and cut out. Roll slab of clay between ⅛-inch lattice strips. Use pattern to cut circle from clay; bore a hanging hole in ornament using a needle and following open circle on pattern for position. Emboss circle with a cross pendant by pressing the cross firmly into the clay. Bake according to clay instructions. Make a hanging loop with white satin ribbon and thread through hole.

The Christbaum

The oldest Christmas tree to be decorated and placed in the parlor is described in a 1605 travel diary by an unidentified visitor to Strasbourg. This traveler saw fir trees hung with paper roses of many different colors, as well as apples, flat wafers, gilded candies, and sugar. In early Christian art, the rose was a symbol for Mary, Jesus' mother, and the flat wafers were the communion symbol for Christ. A tree decorated with these wafers or cookies became known as a *Christbaum*.

The Christbaum Tree

These trees were decorated with roses, a tradition that was rooted in the legend that on the night of Christ's birth, flowers and trees miraculously blossomed the world over. This legend gave rise to the practice of decorating the Christmas tree with paper roses. Through the ages people added their own ideas to the Christbaum. Christ-bundles were hung from the tree—little packets filled with candy, sugarplums, and cakes—reflecting the joyous and generous spirit of Christmas when all gifts came from the Christ child.

In time, pastries began to replace communion wafers as decorations. They were made in two colors: White dough was shaped into flowers, bells, stars, angels, and hearts, while brown dough was used to make figures of men and animals.

Paper Rose Ornaments for a Modern-Day Christbaum

MATERIALS

tissue paper, red or white
florist's wire
green florist's tape

scissors
ruler
pencil

Cut one 3-inch and one 4-inch square of tissue paper. Crumple 3-inch square into a ball; place ball at one corner of 4-inch square. Fold opposite corner of 4-inch square toward ball, sandwiching ball between layers of tissue and forming a triangle. Next, fold other 2 corners of triangle toward ball, then roll and twist folded paper to resemble a tight bud, with crumpled ball at base of bud. Wrap floral wire around base of bud, securing paper. Trace pattern for rose petal 7 times onto tissue paper; cut out 7 petals. Add petals all around bud, one at a time, and with straight bottom edges even with base of bud; wrap with wire to secure. When last petal has been added, make a $1^3/_4$-inch stem with length of doubled wire. Wrap base of flower with florist's tape, covering wiring; continue down to cover stem. Pull tape taut while wrapping; wrap tightly for a firm, straight stem. Twist stem around tree branch.

"White Dough" Pretzels for Modern-Day Christbaum

MATERIALS

cardboard for pattern
white bake-clay

two ¼-inch lattice strips
satin ribbon for hanging

Trace entire pattern of a pretzel onto cardboard. Cut out, including inner sections. Roll slab of clay between ¼-inch lattice strips. Use pattern to cut pretzel shape from clay. Bake according to clay instructions. Thread satin ribbon through bottom hole of pretzel; tie for hanging loop.

Nativity Scene

To remind your children of the true center of Christmas (the baby Jesus) make a hanging nativity scene for the tree using a knobby gourd. Saw off the front of the gourd to make a window for crèche figures. Let your children model these figures from clay.

For the Antique Lover: Unusual Tree Stands

- Place a small tree in an old shopping basket on wheels, or use an old apple basket or woven hamper.

- Use an old enamelware pot or breadbox as a colorful tree stand.

- Turn a rustic stool upside down and allow potted tree to rest between the legs.

- Use old pottery or crocks as a tree stand.

- Use a copper steamer as tree stand.

Pomander Candle Ornaments

Cut room for a tea candle in the top of an orange; use an embroidery needle to pierce a design into orange and press cloves into the holes. Hang the ornament using copper wire.

Spend a restful evening gazing at a small tree full of these lit ornaments, making sure someone is always present while you allow the candles to burn.

Antique Graduated Grain Measures

Stacked one on top of another, these make a nice, tiered, tabletop tree. Decorate the ledges that are formed with laurel leaves, nuts, votive candles, figurines, or any other miniatures of your choice. Top the smallest box with a tiny artificial evergreen to continue the "tree" theme.

Let us now go even unto Bethlehem,
and see this thing which is come to pass,
which the Lord hath made known unto us.

LUKE 2:15

Away in a manger,
no crib for a bed,
The little Lord Jesus laid down His sweet head;
The stars in the bright sky looked down where He lay,
The little Lord Jesus, asleep on the hay.

ANONYMOUS

Trees to Display Antique Collections

- A miniature tree could display an antique button collection. The buttons are easy to thread, and a nice variety of shapes, sizes, and colors would make a pretty tree.

- Antique silver spoons make beautiful decorations. They can be hung, handle down and bowl of spoon toward top, with silver thread tied below the bowl part. Little white lights reflecting off these spoons would be pretty.

- Decorate a small tree with heirloom lace, doilies, or hankies.

- Or decorate a tree with a miniature bottle collection.

Baby Shower Tree

If someone is expecting a baby around Christmas, decorate a tree for a baby shower with little baby necessities: brush and comb sets, safety pins, washcloths, pacifiers, teething rings, etc.

And whoso shall receive
one such little child in my name receiveth me.

MATTHEW 18:5

Wedding Shower Tree

How about a tree that could be decorated for a couple with a Christmas wedding? It could be covered with fanned money, gift certificates, or other small gifts, along with wedding announcements, printed reception napkins, etc.

The Lichstock

About the time evergreens were becoming popular as Christmas trees, a Christmas treelike decoration called a "pyramid" also came into use. Cut evergreen boughs were wrapped around open pyramid-shaped wooden frames, which were then decorated with candles and pastry. This candle-covered tree, called a *lichstock,* eventually developed into the candlelit Christmas tree, but for a long time the *lichstock* and *Christbaum* existed side by side.

Advent Tree

Decorate with key Bible verses that have been decoupaged on glass balls that are hung at intervals as the family reads the story of the birth of the Christ child.

*And the Word was made flesh,
and dwelt among us,
(and we beheld his glory,
the glory as of the only begotten of the Father,)
full of grace and truth.*

JOHN 1:14

Hark, the herald angels sing,
"Glory to the newborn King!"

SAMUEL WESLEY

Doll Clothes Tree

Surprise a little girl who loves Barbies or other small dolls with a small tree in her room hung with doll clothes, instead of, or in addition to, a Christmas stocking.

Baseball Card Tree

For a youngster who likes collecting baseball cards, hang a little tree with baseball cards that have been laminated or placed in sleeves.

Sugartrees

Trees in the eighteenth century were decorated with many kinds of sweet confections, as well as apples and fruits and nuts. They were often called "sugartrees." On the evening of Twelfth Night or Epiphany, January 6, which commemorates the arrival of the Magi at Bethlehem, the sugartrees were shaken and the sweets eaten.

Memory Tree

If your children have all grown up and moved away, how about decorating two trees: one fancy one and one Memory Tree that holds all the ornaments constructed by your children over the years?

Southwestern Tree

For those who live in the Southwest and are proud of their heritage, how about a tree decorated with chili peppers, cacti, minisaddles, boots, cowboy hats, burros, Indian teepees, and Indian drums? There are entire websites devoted to selling Southwestern Christmas decorations.

The Seamstress's Tree

Decorate your tree with small sewing items, such as thimbles, spools, and silver scissors.

Father Christmas Tree

There are many, many different Santa ornaments made from so many different materials and springing from so many different national heritages. To keep your perspective, remember to include my favorite—the old saint bowing beside the manger to the Christ child.

Lamb Tree

Cover a tree with different types of lambs, to remind you of the One whose birthday we celebrate.

Behold the Lamb of God,
which taketh away the sin of the world.

JOHN 1:29

Children's Theme Trees

Children enjoy trees with one theme. Here are some decoration possibilities:

animals	dolls
toys	dime-store gifts
fairy-tale characters	"jewels"
snowflakes	birds
bells	buttons and bows
stars	

English Christmas Trees

Queen Victoria's husband, Prince Albert, who came from the German province of Saxe-Coburg, is generally credited with introducing the Christmas tree to England after the birth of their first son in 1841. The origin of the story about Prince Albert's connection with Christmas trees may have been a full-page illustration in an 1848 edition of the *Illustrated London News* showing one of Albert's trees at Windsor. Because Victorians often imitated the royal family, the custom spread rapidly.

This motley collection of odd objects,
clustering on the tree like magic fruit
. . .made lively realisation of
the fancies of childhood;
and set me thinking
how all the trees that grow
and all the things that
come into existence on the earth,
have their wild adornments
at that well-remembered time.

CHARLES DICKENS

Care of the Tree

If the needles feel rubbery and alive, and if the cut end exudes a gummy, sticky substance, the tree will be reasonably fresh. Avoid trees whose needles have turned brown in spots or that fall when shaken gently. Trees with a trunk length from seven to ten inches below the lowest usable branch will need to be recut for placement.

Allow your tree to remain outdoors, protected from the sun until ready for use. Rain and snow are good for it, or you may spray the whole tree once or twice to keep the needles moist. Recut the trunk on a deep diagonal before placing in the stand to expose as much surface for water consumption as possible. Add either of the following to the water as a stimulant: 1 cup of sugar, molasses, or syrup, or 1 teaspoonful of plant fertilizer, to each quart of water.

Do not take the tree directly into your heated room from outside. Instead, take it first to a cool basement for a day, then move it to its final location. A gradual transition will be less of a shock and will help prolong its beauty and life.

Set the Mood

BLUE TREE LIGHTS:
make us think of a cold frosty night;

WHITE TREE LIGHTS: imply purity;

MULTICOLORED TREE LIGHTS: are gay and festive.

Create a Winter Scene

As an under-the-tree decoration, cover stacked books or magazines with a white sheet and cotton batting. Create scenes with skiers, skaters, churchgoers, wise men, shepherds, etc. Children will particularly enjoy arranging and rearranging the scene.

Primitive Trees

For trees with a primitive feeling, fireproofed straw makes a great undertree treatment and reminds us of Christ's humble birth. Emphasize the natural beauty of the tree by making ropes or garlands of acorns, walnuts, hazelnuts, peanuts, and almonds. Hang straw figures, and instead of stringing lights on this tree, emphasize the subtle coloring of the decorations using a green or yellow reflector flood lamp of 150 watts.

The Ceppo Tree

Francis of Assisi, attempting to make the story of Christ's birth more understandable to the people of the Italian countryside, was the first to use small carved figures to depict the characters. The idea appealed to the people, and they, in turn, carved similar figures to relate the story to their children. These early nativity scenes evolved into pyramid-shaped structures that contained several shelves on which the nativity figures were placed. Above them were small trinkets and figurines of animals, birds, and angels. The figures were collected or made with loving care and handed down from generation to generation.

Piñata Tree

Make small piñatas in the form of bells, stars, animals, and balls from fabric, felt, or foil paper. Cut 2 pieces of each design and sew, glue, or staple them together. Decorate with paper streamers, faces, and comical hats. Fill with fancy candies, nuts, miniature toys, and flowers.

Then fill 5-inch squares of colored cellophane with confetti. Draw up the corners of the cellophane squares and tie with a 9-inch length of ribbon. Allow the ends of the cellophane to extend above the ribbon to resemble flower petals.

Next shape #10 wire into a pyramid-shaped tree. Wire a length of 1-inch hemp rope to this form and paint it red. Suspend the tree from the ceiling by a rope fastened to the top, allowing enough rope to swing tree back and forth and to raise and lower it. Tie the gift piñatas and the confetti piñatas to the tips of the wire "branches." At midnight, tell each Christmas guest to grab 1 cellophane piñata from the tree, which you have set in motion. After the confetti piñatas are broken, each person in turn then tries to claim a gift piñata from the swinging tree.

The Dog's Tree

Children will enjoy creating a special tree for a favorite pet. Ask the butcher for extra bones and hang them on the tree with dog toys, biscuits, and other canine yummies.

Advent Tree

To make a tree decoration for your door, cut a tree form, trunk, and base from plywood and a similar shape from $1/2$-inch mesh hardware cloth. Tack the hardware cloth to the plywood. Rub the trunk with brown shoe polish. Cut 4-inch lengths of arborvitae and weave them into the mesh openings. Make sure your tree and base are well filled and present a rounded appearance. Hang miniature figures, animals, or toys on the tree. When children visit tell them to select and take home a figure. Of course, you will need to redecorate often, but the tree will be fun for all.

American Christmas Trees

Tree trimming was not widely practiced in the United States until after the Civil War. Here, as abroad, the first trees were small enough to be set on tables. Initially, Christmas trees were hung with edibles, but by 1860 city folk could purchase special toys and imported glass ornaments. Families living in rural areas exercised their ingenuity and contrived tree ornaments out of spare materials. Favorite decorations included candles, cookies, popcorn strings, gilded walnuts, candy-filled cornucopias, blown and colored eggs, paper chains and cutouts, baskets, small flags, simple toys, carvings, and little gifts.

Christmas Dinner Table Tree

Use round or oval mirror for the base. Cut 4-inch lengths of yew and wire them to a wrought iron candle tree with #25 wire. Start at the tips and work toward the center by placing three 4-inch lengths of yew on the frame. Bind with #32 wire. Place a second group of yew on the frame, making sure to overlap the stems of the previous placement. Continue in this manner until the tree is covered. Trim slightly if needed. Place red candles in the holders and stand the tree on the mirror. Tuck short lengths of greens under the mirror base. Add small nativity figures at the base.

The Yew Sleigh Tree

This tree can be made from several branches of yew assembled to resemble a tree. Place a pinpoint in the bottom of a miniature table-top sleigh. Wedge a good-sized potato on the pinpoint and insert the yew into the potato. The moisture in the potato will keep the greens fresh. Decorate the tree with red berries thrust into the greens and potato. Place gifts near the sleigh.

Designs from Plant Materials

The seedpods from many flowers such as iris, yucca, oriental poppy, goldenrod, rose hips, buckwheat blossoms, milkweed pods, sumac berries, and eucalyptus pods can be used as ornaments. They are lovely in their natural state or they can be gilded, silvered, or painted. Pinecones add interesting variety of design. Try cutting through the cone with a sharp knife or small saw to form rosettes that resemble flowers. The stem end is especially interesting. Paint, gild, silver, or use in their natural state. Wind wires around the segments so they cannot be seen and use to hang.

An American Tradition

In 1900, only one out of every five American families had a Christmas tree. Most children, however, probably enjoyed one at school or at a neighbor's house—and all children wished for a tree of their own. By 1910, in most parts of America, their dream had come true—nearly every family had a tree at home. And by 1930, the Christmas tree had become an American tradition.

Egg Shell Ornaments

Punch a pinhole in the top and the bottom of the shell. Blow gently through one end so that the contents are expelled. Wash the shell, and let dry thoroughly. Paint any color you like and decorate with sequins, beads, paper stripping, bits of felt, and paper. Funny heads can be made by painting in features or pasting on paper eyes, noses, and mouths. Glue perky paper hats to the top of the head.

Mirror Plaques for the Tree

Paint designs on pocket mirrors with poster paint. With glue, add beads, paper stripping, angel hair, bits of scouring pads, and cotton. With pinking shears cut a backing of felt 1 inch larger than the dimensions of the mirror. Place a strip of ribbon between the felt and the mirror. Glue the mirror to the felt.

Jesse Tree

This is a special tree that reminds children of the Old Testament stories that pointed to the coming of Christ. You may want to use a smaller Christmas tree for this, or even a large houseplant. Each ornament for the tree symbolizes an Old Testament story; for instance, a ladder represents Jacob; little tablets, the law of Moses; a rainbow, the story of Noah; a harp for David; a trumpet for the walls of Jericho; a sheaf of wheat for Ruth and Naomi; a scroll, Isaiah's prophecy; and so on. Use your knowledge of the Bible to come up with your own ornament ideas, and ask your children for their help. Each night of Advent, tell an Old Testament story and have a child hang on the Jesse Tree the ornament that goes with that story. This will help children understand the connection between Christ's coming and the Old Testament.

The Giving Tree

Have a small second Christmas tree in your house where throughout Advent children can place gifts for the needy. (Or you could do this activity at church for Sunday school classes or groups.) They might want to use their own spending money to buy gifts, or they can wrap new toys that they would like to share with someone who has less than they have. At the end of Advent, go together as a group to deliver the gifts to a local shelter or other charity.

Trimming the Tree

This activity takes the hassle out of decorating the tree. After you set up your Christmas tree, leave it bare except for the lights. Place the ornaments in a box beside the tree. Then each time a child does an act that expresses the true spirit of Christmas, he or she gets to hang a decoration on the tree. (Obviously, the decorations will need to be "child friendly.") Your tree may not end up looking like Martha Stewart decorated it. But it will be a testament to your children's love and goodwill for one another.

Their Very Own Trees

Young children often like to redecorate the tree every day. Here's an idea that avoids adult frustration and allows children to redecorate to their hearts' content. Cut small branches from shrubbery or use branches trimmed off of your Christmas tree. Place the branches in a large can filled with gravel. Then give the children an assortment of unbreakable decorations and place each child's "tree" in his or her bedroom. As they grow older, you can let them put lights on the branches as well. They'll spend a lot of time in their rooms simply watching their "trees."

Taking Down the Tree

The old-fashioned edible Christmas tree decorations gave children a pleasure to anticipate that has been lost today. In the past, all through the holidays the tantalizing cookies and candies that hung on the tree were forbidden fruit; they had to stay in place until the tree was taken down on Twelfth Night, when they could finally be eaten. Back then, taking down the tree was not the dismal, anticlimactic chore it is today; instead, it was the much awaited, delicious climax to the Christmas season.

Modern-day families may not want to encourage an orgy of sweets—but to make taking down the tree a little less painful, wrap a few small extra gifts and hide them among the tree's branches, to be opened after all the dismantling is complete. Wrap these after-Christmas presents in gold paper, as "gifts of gold" are part of the Epiphany tradition, in remembrance of the wise men's gifts to the Christ child.

Family Tree

MATERIALS

18-inch-long paper-covered wire
(for example, 36 pieces for
18 family members)
boxwood leaves
1½-inch photo of each family
member

glue
dried flowers
ribbon
6 x 6-inch piece of
1½-inch thick
green Styrofoam
sheet moss

Begin by twisting together all of the pieces of covered wire about 2 inches from the bottom and continue upwards about 6 inches. Fan the bottom pieces out to form the "roots" of the tree. At the top of the twist, begin to divide the "branches" into groups of 4, fanning them out on both sides of the tree. Separate the strands of each group of 4 and fan out also. Trim ends of branches with scissors when finished to achieve realistic tree shape. Glue a 2-inch ribbon loop to each photo. Then glue around perimeter of each photo and sprinkle with dried flowers to create frame effect. Cover Styrofoam with sheet moss and stick roots of tree in Styrofoam. Glue boxwood leaves to tree branches to simulate an evergreen tree and hang photos of family members to tree in generational order.

Alternative Christmas Tree

MATERIALS

glossy evergreen clippings,
  such as boxwood
rose hips
false berries
damp sphagnum moss
1-inch wire mesh netting

wire cutters
7-inch-diameter
  flowerpot
florist's adhesive tape
scissors
florist's scissors

Place the moss on the wire mesh netting and turn corners into center to enclose, crushing into a ball shape. Place ball in the flowerpot and secure with 2 or 3 pieces of adhesive tape. Cut evergreens to approximately equal lengths and push stems in the wire ball until completely filled in. Push in rose hips and false berries.

Advent for the Birds

At the beginning of December have the kids string popcorn and cranberries for a "bird's Christmas tree." They can also decorate the tree with pinecones covered with cheap peanut butter and then rolled in birdseed. This activity reminds children that God's love and care extend even to the natural world around us.

Surprise Rolls for the Tree

MATERIALS

cardboard tubing from wrapping paper, paper towels,
waxed paper, aluminum foil, or toilet tissue
brightly colored crepe paper
long piece of ribbon for curling
assorted candies, treats, and snacks

Cut tubes into equal-length sections (about 3½ inches long). Place the cardboard tube on paper and roll up, pinching paper together at one end and tying with a piece of curling ribbon. Fill tube with treats, pinch other end, and tie with more curling ribbon. Open twisted ends, and decorate with glue and glitter or Christmas stickers.

Kissing Ball Ornaments

(for tree or hanging in doorways)

MATERIALS

2 wooden embroidery hoops	ribbons, trim, or beads
glue gun	mistletoe
glue sticks	

Crisscross wooden embroidery hoops, placing one inside the other, so they are perpendicular, and glue together. Decorate with ribbons, trim, or beads and place sprig of mistletoe in the center. Tie a ribbon at the top for hanging.

Gingerbread-Friends Garland

MATERIALS

clay gingerbread men
red and white icing
1/8-inch red ribbon

red and white icing
scissors

Using oven-bake clay, make a batch of gingerbread men. Punch holes in each hand with a drinking straw and bake. After the "cookies" have cooled, outline and decorate using icing. Link the men together by threading thin ribbon through holes in their hands. Knot ribbon and trim the ends.

Heart-Sachet Tree Ornaments

MATERIALS

fabric
pinking shears
thread

potpourri
ribbon

Cut 2 pieces of fabric (cut through 2 layers at once) with pinking shears in the shape of a heart. With wrong sides of fabric together, machine-stitch around heart close to pinked edge, spooning in a tablespoon of potpourri when half sewn. Finish sewing and attach a ribbon loop to hang from tree.

Metal Foil Ornaments

MATERIALS

metal foil, in brass, copper, and aluminum (available from craft stores)

ballpoint pen

metallic thread (for hanging)

Draw a shape onto stiff paper and cut it out to create a pattern. Put the pattern on a piece of metal foil that is slightly larger than the pattern, and draw around it using a soft pencil. Place the foil on a pile of magazines with the pattern on top in the same position; remove ink cartridge from a ballpoint pen and go over the outline with the empty pen to draw freehand within the outline to create details, remembering to press hard all the time. Use a pair of strong scissors to cut out the design and pierce a hole at the top. Tie a loop of metallic thread through for hanging. Flatten foil gently with rolling pin if it has curled. The right side is the opposite side to the one worked on, which gives the metal a raised, "embossed" effect.

A Great Invention

Christmas tree hooks were one of the greatest inventions in Christmas tree history. They were first advertised in a wholesaler's catalogue in 1892:

> *It is a well-known fact, that heretofore it has taken the best part of Christmas Eve to trim a tree by tying strings or threads to the trinkets, and then tying these to the tree, thus taking about 2 to 3 hours of one person's time and labor to trim a tree with 100 articles. With these hooks, the same number can be applied in less than half an hour.*

Lace-Embossed Clay Tree Ornaments

MATERIALS

modeling compound clay

luncheon-sized plate

masking tape

piece of old lace or paper doilies

talcum powder

1 x 8-inch dowel rod

small straw

gold or silver thread

On a protected surface, tape luncheon plate facedown and lightly dust with talcum powder. Roll a 1-inch ball of modeling clay to an even thickness in the center of the plate using the dowel rod. Place lace or doily over the clay and roll again to emboss pattern into the clay. Remove lace and push straw through top of the ornament to form a hole through which metallic thread may be strung to hang ornament. These ornaments may also be painted.

Nature's Ornaments

- Place orange rings cut in $\frac{1}{4}$-inch slices on an oven rack at lowest temperature and dry for 1 hour. Just below the peel, push a hole through with knife tip and thread with a ribbon and tie to tree.

- Bundle together 3 or 4 cinnamon sticks with a pretty ribbon and glue cranberries to the ribbon with a glue gun; place bundle on tree branches.

- Thread tiny kumquats onto medium stub wires and loop circlets over tree branches or tie with contrasting ribbons.

- Tie ribbon or yarn around top petals of a pinecone for hanging, and glue beads on cone as ornaments.

Matzebaum

In the nineteenth century, the Pennsylvania Germans decorated their trees with *matzebaum,* wafer-thin, 2 x 4-inch cakes made from almond paste, sugar, and egg whites. Before being baked, each cake was pressed with a carved wooden mold that left raised images of animals, birds, or flowers on the face of the cookie. After baking, matzebaum were usually painted with homemade vegetable dyes. Most of the cookies were eaten by the children when the Christmas tree was dismantled, but a few were laid away and brought out to decorate the family tree year after year.

Thicker objects—vegetables, fruits, and animals—were also shaped from the same type of almond-flavored dough and called marzipan or marchpane. Marzipan originated in Persia and had been made in Germany since the Middle Ages. It was originally a delicacy consumed at court banquets and became a common Christmas confection during the eighteenth century.

Marzipan Potatoes

MATERIALS

MARZIPAN:

1 lb. pure almond paste

1½ c. sifted confectioners' sugar

3 tbsp. light corn syrup

¾ tsp. vanilla

ALSO:

cinnamon

toothpick

needle

gold thread for hanging

Mix marzipan ingredients together and knead until smooth. Break off pieces of marzipan and roll into 1-inch-diameter shapes resembling potatoes; do not make balls perfectly round. When satisfied with shape, roll in cinnamon. Insert toothpick through one end of each potato for hanging hole. Allow potatoes to harden, then thread needle with 7-inch length of gold thread. Run needle and thread through hanging hole; knot ends.

Edible Decorations

*A*nother cookie hung on the Christmas tree was the white *springerle,* made of an egg dough seasoned with anise seeds. The smooth dough produced an excellent cameolike image when molded, and the cookies were often painted and then hung from the tree with a piece of string or a ribbon. Most of the molds were the work of professional German woodcarvers, and few families possessed these fancy cookie molds. Most households, though, had cookie cutters made by itinerant tinsmiths.

Springerles

INGREDIENTS

3¼ c. flour
¼ tsp. baking powder
4 large eggs
1⅔ c. sugar

1 tsp. finely grated lemon zest
1 tsp. anise extract
optional: 2–3 tbsp. whole
or crushed anise seeds

Roll out the dough ¼-inch thick, using extra flour to keep the dough from sticking. Press molds firmly into dough, and then cut cookies apart with a knife. Sprinkle with anise seeds if desired. Use a spatula to transfer cookies to a greased baking sheet, ½ inch apart. (If cookies are to be used as a decoration, use a straw to take out a circle of dough where a loop can be inserted for hanging.) Set the cookies aside for 10–12 hours, and then bake at 300° F for 18–25 minutes, until the cookies are almost firm but not colored. If desired, decorate the cookies with a paintbrush and a wash made out of diluted food coloring. Insert yarn or ribbon loops and hang on the tree. Springerles are meant to be very hard, and they keep indefinitely. They will still be edible at the end of the Christmas season when you take down the tree.

Sugar Ring Cookies to Hang on the Tree

MATERIALS

dough (see recipe following)
compass
paper for pattern

darning needle
red or green yarn or ribbons
for hanging

Preheat oven to 350° F. On paper draw 2 concentric circles ¾ inch and 2¼ inches in diameter. Cut around outer circle, then inner, leaving ring pattern. Roll out ball of dough to ⅛-inch thickness. Place ring pattern on dough and trace around edges with knife or darning needle; remove pattern. Repeat until all dough is used. Place cookies on sheets; leave plain or coat with colored sprinkles, tapping sprinkles lightly into the dough with the tip of your finger. Bake for 8–10 minutes or until golden brown. Cool on rack. For each cookie, cut 7-inch length of yarn or ribbon; thread through center of ring and knot ends.

DOUGH RECIPE

½ c. softened butter or margarine
½ c. sugar
2 eggs
½ tsp. vanilla

1½ c. flour
¾ tsp. double-acting baking
powder
¼ tsp. salt

Combined softened butter or margarine and sugar and beat until creamy. Add eggs and vanilla, beating well. Add flour, baking powder, and salt; beat until well mixed. Form into ball and chill for 3 hours.

Cookie Decorations

Most of the cookies on nineteenth-century Christmas trees—spice, butter, and gingerbread—were thicker than today's cookies, often half an inch thick. Cookie-baking binges lasted for two solid weeks early in December. A "washbasketful" was a standard measure of cookies in Pennsylvania-Dutch kitchens. The housewife who didn't have at least several washbaskets full of cookies just wasn't ready for Christmas. And many of these went on the tree.

By the 1880s, in addition to gingerbread animals and people, flat gingerbread cakes were hung on the trees. They were decorated with colorful pictures pasted on with egg white.

Icing

(for cookie decorations)

2 egg whites   1¼ c. confectioners' sugar
⅜ tsp. cream of tartar

Beat egg whites with whisk or electric beater until frothy and slightly thickened. Add cream of tartar and continue beating until whites hold a peak. Sift confectioners' sugar into whites, about ½ cup at a time, beating thoroughly between additions. Beat 5–8 minutes until icing is thick and smooth.

Cookies with Paper Cutouts to Hang on the Tree

MATERIALS

Dough and Icing
(see recipes on pages 72–73)
ruler
paper for pattern
knife
darning needle

prints of angels or other
motifs from
Christmas cards
curved cuticle scissors
paintbrush for icing
gold ribbon

Preheat oven to 325° F. On paper, draw a rectangle 3¼ x 4 inches; round the corners. Cut out pattern. Roll out dough between sheets of wax paper to ½-inch thickness. Place pattern on dough and trace around edges with knife or darning needle; remove pattern. Punch small hanging hole near center top of one short edge. Repeat until all dough is used. Place cookies on sheets. Bake for 35 minutes or until cookies are firm and brown. Cool completely. While cookies are baking and cooling, carefully cut out prints using curved cuticle scissors. When cookies are cool, cover the back of the print with a thin layer of icing. Press the iced side of the print on the center of the cookie. Thread hanging hole with gold ribbon; knot ends.

Gingerbread Dough

(for cookie decorations)

6 c. flour
4 tsp. ground ginger
1 1/2 tsp. ground cinnamon
1 tsp. ground cloves
1/4 tsp. each: ground nutmeg,
    cardamom, salt

2 sticks butter or
    margarine
1 c. firmly packed light
    brown sugar
1/2 c. dark corn syrup
1/2 c. light molasses

Sift flour and spices together in bowl. Combine butter, brown sugar, corn syrup, and molasses in saucepan and place over low heat until butter is melted and all ingredients are blended. Remove from heat. Combine 2 cups flour mixture and the butter mixture in mixing bowl and blend well. Continue adding remaining flour mixture, blending until dough is firm but pliable. Flour hands and knead dough until smooth and slightly sticky. If dough is too moist, add flour by the tablespoon. Refrigerate for 1 hour.

Stuffed Animal Ornaments

MATERIALS

animal cookie cutters or pattern
pencil
fabric—cotton, calico, felt, wool, suede cloth, leather
straight pins
scissors or pinking shears

sewing needle
colored thread
fiberfill, cotton batting, or shredded nylon stockings
colored yarn, buttons, or any other trim desired

Make a pattern by tracing a cookie cutter directly onto the fabric; trace a cardboard pattern, or draw a figure of your own, such as simple elephants, sheep, horses, chickens, and ducks. Pin the pattern onto a double layer of fabric. If the material will be sewn on the wrong side and turned right side out, add an additional ¼ inch to the pattern. With scissors or pinking shears, cut out the 2 layers of fabric along these lines. Sew the right sides together ¼ inch from the edge. Leave a 1-inch space open to insert the stuffing. Trim seam edges, turn right side out, and stuff with fiberfill, stockings, or other lightweight filler. Stitch up the stuffing hole. Add eyes (buttons may be used), tail, swings, or mane using scraps of fabric or yarn. Sew on a thread loop for hanging the ornament.

Christmas tree decorations do not need to be expensive. Our ancestors made most of their decorations from things they found in the natural world around them. The next few pages contain instructions for ornaments that you, too, can make from items you find in nature (or purchase from craft stores if the outdoor world isn't handy for you).

Starfish Decorations

MATERIALS

dried starfish (can be purchased
at most craft stores or at
a beach store)

scissors
lightweight clear plastic
fishing line

Wrap thin lightweight fishing line around the starfish as a hanger. Tie securely and hang.

Sand Dollar Decorations

MATERIALS

sand dollars (collected from the
beach or purchased from
craft or beach store)

red or green satin ribbon,
$1/4$ inch wide
Christmas tree hanger

If you collect sand dollars on the beach, dry them thoroughly and then soak them in a strong bleach solution (3 parts bleach to 1 part water) for a day or until they are white. Rinse thoroughly with water and dry in the sun. Sand dollars are extremely fragile and must be handled with great care. When completely dry, tie a satin bow through the center hole in the sand dollar. Attach a tree hanger to the bow.

Pinecone Angel

MATERIALS

heavy scissors or flower clippers
3-inch pinecone
2 dried milkweed pods
    (gather them in the fall)
white glue
black felt pen with a fine point
hickory nut, small
    walnut, or other nut
    about $\frac{1}{4}$-inch high
small piece of string or
    yarn for hanger

Cut off the top bracts (petals) from the pinecone to make room for the angel's head, which is the nut. Take the milkweed pods, hollow side facing out, and push into the back of the cone to form wings. Glue and let dry. Make facial features on the nut head with the black felt pen, then glue it onto the cone. When dry, glue on a hanger of string or yarn.

Cornhusk Flower Decoration

MATERIALS

field corn with shucks attached

boiling water in a pan or kettle

knife or cleaver

scissors

Gather field corn in the fall after the first frost has turned the ears of corn down. Be careful to leave 2 to 3 inches of stem. Pull back the husks, exposing the entire ear. Using a knife or cleaver, cut away all but the last $1/2$ inch of the ear, leaving approximately 3 rows of kernels, which will be used for the center of the flower. Return the husks to their original position, and cut each of them with the scissors to resemble petals. Carefully work over a kettle of boiling water and shape each petal with your hands. The steam makes the petals very pliable. The longer the husks are, the larger the flowers will be.

Popcorn and Red Pepper String

MATERIALS

sturdy white thread
long sewing needle
dried red peppers, 1 to 2
  inches long

freshly popped white popcorn,
  unsalted and unbuttered
  (One large bowl makes a
  makes a 5-foot chain.)

Thread the needle and put it through 1 red pepper either lengthwise or widthwise. Tie the thread securely around the pepper to form a knot. Thread the popcorn onto the string alternating peppers and popcorn. You can use 1 pepper to every 6 to 12 pieces of popcorn or alternate popcorn and peppers. Make the chain as long as you like. However, if it is over 6 feet long, the chain becomes difficult to handle. Several chains can be tied together before putting them on the tree. Only freshly popped corn should be used, because stale popcorn tends to shatter.

Corn Shuck Pig Decoration

MATERIALS

3-inch-long ear of corn, such
    as a small ear of popcorn, with
    the husks still attached
knife

water
straight pin
white glue
thread

Carefully remove the corncob, but leave the husks attached to the base. Trim off all but 2½ inches from the pointed end of the corncob and remove the kernels of corn. Dampen the husks. Slip the cob inside the husks, pointed end first. Pull the ends of the husks together and twist or braid them. Curl to form a tail. Secure with a pin until dry enough to glue together. Trim the base end of the corn shuck to form a snout. Cut a cornstalk in 4 equal lengths for legs. Be sure they are in proportion to the body. Glue them to the dry body. Cut a shorter cornstalk and split it to make 2 ears. Glue in place. Note: You may need to tie a bit of thread around the nose if the husks come loose from the base.

Black Walnut Owl Ornament

MATERIALS

2 medium-sized black walnut shells
small wire brush
pliers or bench vise
small hand or electric saw
straight pin
medium-grade sandpaper or file

household cement
tiny eye screw
metal or yarn hanger
optional—hand or
    electric drill

Select medium-sized black walnut shells. You will need ½ shell for the head and a whole walnut for the body. Note: Regular walnuts cannot be used. Clean the shells with a wire brush. Cut 1 shell into 2 equal parts following the seam line as closely as possible. To cut, place the shell in a bench vise and saw with either a handsaw or an electric saw. Or hold the shell with pliers and feed it into the saw blade very slowly. (Don't try to hold the shell in your hand; you may cut your finger.)

Clean out the meat from the split walnut with a straight pin. Sand the cut side of this shell to eliminate saw marks. Sand the top of the whole shell and the bottom of the half shell to obtain the smooth surface needed for gluing together. The bottom of the body can also be sanded smooth to allow the owl to stand alone. Using a vise to hold the head, drill a small hole for an eye screw at the top of head. Glue the head to the body with household cement and let it set for about 10 hours. Add a metal or yarn hanger. You can drill small holes in the back of the head through the eye holes to allow light to shine through.

Shell Wreath

(to hang on the tree or door)

Materials

X-acto knife or sturdy scissors
corrugated cardboard (4 inches x
    4 inches x ¼-inch thick—
    2 thin pieces can be glued
    together)

household cement
red velvet ribbon, ¼-inch
    wide and 24 inches long
shells in assorted sizes

With the X-acto knife or the scissors, cut the cardboard into a circle 4 inches in diameter, then cut a circle 2 inches in diameter out of the center. Glue a piece of the velvet ribbon around the outside edge of the circle. Glue the rest of the ribbon through the center and tie it into a bow for a hanger.

Using shells picked up at the beach, or purchased, start at the top of the circle and glue on 1 of the larger shells. Glue other larger shells around the edges at well-spaced intervals. Then put in shells of all kinds, textures, sizes, and colors to form a pleasing pattern. Use pieces of spiral cord and tiny shells to fill in any gaps. No 2 wreaths will be alike.

Hemlock String

MATERIALS

long, sharp needle
lightweight clear plastic fishing line

dried hemlock cones

Thread the needle and push it through 1 hemlock cone. Tie the fishing line firmly around the first cone to secure it. Thread the rest of the cones onto the fishing line and secure the last cone as you did the first. String the cones through the middle or end to end. Make the chain as long as you wish.

Acorn Box Ornament

Remove the cap from a newly fallen acorn. Carve out the white circle underneath and remove the soft meat from inside the acorn. Wrap fine-grade sandpaper around a pencil eraser and smooth the inside of the acorn shell. Stain the outside with wood stain and allow to dry overnight. Select a cork that fits snugly into the acorn cap. Shorten the cork and carve to fit into the acorn opening. Smooth the cork with sandpaper and glue into cap. Drill a hole through the acorn's stem, and attach a loop of ribbon.

Topiaries

Topiaries are a variety of tabletop Christmas tree. The custom of training plants to grow in topiary form originated with the Romans and was more recently popular with the Victorians, who created topiaries from wire and filled them with moss, greenery, and flowers. Place topiaries where they can be enjoyed close-up—on sideboards, mantels, or tabletops. Fill them with oranges, lady apples, limes, and pomegranates. For greenery, use whatever you find in your backyard: pine, spruce, ivy, or holly. Use an interesting vase, garden accessory, or pottery bowl as a pedestal.

Lemon Topiary

MATERIALS

length of chicken wire
small, white-painted pinecones
    available at craft stores or
    floral shops

craft foam cone
bundle of florist's picks
fresh lemons
laurel leaves

Wrap the length of chicken wire around the cone from top to bottom to support the weight of the lemons. Nestle the wire-covered cone in a sturdy container, such as a moss-blanketed terra-cotta pot. Arrange the lemons on the cone in circular rows, working from the base to the tip and pressing the lemons into the foam with the florist's picks. In the same way, fill in the tree with pinecones, randomly spacing them along the lemons. For a green flourish, tuck in fresh laurel sprigs, allowing them to fan over the lemons and the pinecones.

A Kitchen Tree

Since so many holiday activities take place in the kitchen, this room deserves its own special tree. Place a little evergreen in a safe little nook of your kitchen and decorate it with dainty lady apples. Just slightly larger than sugarplums, they create a simple and beautiful tree and can be hung from golden metallic ribbon hangers secured to the apples with straight pins.

Rosemary Trees

Another decoration for the kitchen, the Rosemary Tree is both useful and lovely. Training these little trees takes some time and patience, though. Plant a straight-rooted cutting of rosemary in a pot of sterile, prepackaged soil. Place a stake in the soil by the plant. Loosely secure the plant to the stake with twist ties or raffia. When the plant reaches the desired height, clip the branches of a medium-sized plant into the familiar Christmas tree shape. To maintain, keep in sunlight, turning every few days for even growth. Keep plants moist but be sure not to overwater.

Sandpaper Man and Reindeer

MATERIALS

coarse sandpaper
pencil
strong scissors
white glue
felt scraps—red, green, blue,
   white, and black

scraps of green
   medium-sized rickrack
yarn
cotton

Trace the outlines of the man and reindeer on the smooth sides of 2 pieces of sandpaper. Cut out both shapes and glue the smooth sides together. Let dry. Decorate as follows: Use felt for eyes, mouth, hat, trousers, and belt, rickrack for suspenders, yarn in strips for bangs under the hat, and cotton for a beard. Decorate both sides. Make a yarn loop at the top of the hat for a hanger. Give the reindeer a cotton tail, a harness made out of rickrack or yarn, an eye of black felt, and a red felt nose.

Clustered Glass Balls

Recycle small, faded glass Christmas balls by stringing three or four different colors together on a strand of wire and add a few decorative leaves.

Paper Silhouettes Garland

MATERIALS

colored construction paper   scissors
pencil

Decide which figure you want to make. You can make a string of animals, such as bears or elephants, or a set of figures, such as angels or snowmen. Fold the construction paper into several layers wide enough to accommodate the figure you have chosen and thick enough to make the chain the length you desire. On the folded construction paper, trace the pattern given or draw around your favorite cookie cutter. Cut out the figure, being careful to leave part of the folded area on each side of the shape intact. If the folds are cut through entirely, the figures will not form a chain and will instead be separate and unattached to one another. After the cutting is completed, open the paper figures and find a chain to surround the tree!

Fruitful Trees

Using contrasting colors of sheer organdy, wrap dried oranges, other lightweight commercially freeze-dried fruit, or millinery fruit (cherries, blueberries, pears, apples, grapes, etc.,) with two 12-inch-long pieces and tie together with a satin ribbon to hang from the tree.

Feather Trees

This Christmas decoration was created by the Germans, who loved to celebrate the holiday in a variety of delightful ways. Heavy wire branches were wrapped with feathers, usually from turkeys or geese, and sometimes swans. The feathers were dyed a dark green, giving the branches a natural look.

The first feather trees probably arrived in this country with German immigrants. Most measured from 2½ to 3 feet in height with collapsible wire branches and would have been easily transported in steamer trunks. By the turn of the century, American department stores and mail-order catalogs were offering feather trees for sale. The passage of time brought variations to the details of the feather trees. They became available with different colored or shaped bases, as well as different colors for the feathers and berries. By the end of World War II, trees with built-in electric lights became available. By the 1950s, however, most stores and catalogs no longer sold feather trees, since the development of cellophane, as well as Visca, a dark green strawlike rayon, entered the artificial tree marketplace. But because of the soaring interest in American folk art and vintage holiday decorations, rare vintage feather trees are highly valued, fetching as much as one hundred dollars per foot or more!

Tree Farming

In 1909, the Forest Service estimated that five million Christmas trees were cut, and Christmas tree critics became more vocal every year until by the 1920s conservationists had a well-organized campaign. The Christmas tree trade had been buying the rights to evergreens along the roadsides and then felling every tree in sight, but now they finally realized that they were bringing a lot of criticism on themselves by cutting only the trees that were the easiest to get to market. The cutters began to thin rather than to level the trees along the highways, and sound conservation practices became more prevalent.

Christmas tree cultivation became a profitable business in many parts of the country. Farmers found it a good way to use rocky upland pastures and pieces of land not suited to other farming. In the 1930s, Franklin D. Roosevelt was the country's best-known Christmas tree farmer. He helped popularize the concept by growing Christmas trees on his estate at Hyde Park, New York.

Musical Tree

Hang the branches with miniature instruments, musical scales, and treble and G clefs.

Queen Anne's Lace Tree

Use dried Queen Anne's lace blossoms to decorate a Christmas tree. The blossoms can be picked in various stages of development for variety. Lovely in their natural state, the dried flowers can also be sprayed with white, gold, or silver paint.

Electric Christmas

The frustrating and dangerous problem of the Christmas tree candle was that it would not stand perfectly upright, no matter how carefully the tree trimmer tried to place it on a bough. In 1882, just three years after the invention of the electric lightbulb, the world's first electrically lighted Christmas tree was decorated in New York City at the home of Edward Johnson, a colleague of Thomas Edison.

Spruce Saplings

These young trees make thoughtful, environment-friendly gifts to give to holiday guests. Place a waterproof saucer on a large unfinished square of burlap. Set a tree, still in its nursery pot, onto the saucer. Gather the burlap around the pot and tie it in place with a festive ribbon bow. Then top with gilded stars. Assemble the saplings on your buffet to create your own little grove of trees.

Mossy Tabletop Trees

MATERIALS

plaster of paris
large stick for use as the trunk
terra-cotta pot
craft foam cone
florist's tape

spray adhesive
sheet moss
plastic bucket to be
   concealed in the
   pot

Mix the plaster of paris according to the package directions. Quickly pour the plaster mixture into the plastic bucket. Before the plaster hardens, insert the stick trunk into the center of the bucket; hold the trunk upright with a brace of florist's tape until the plaster completely hardens. Coat the top of the cone with spray adhesive. Press small, easy-to-manage pieces of sheet moss onto the adhesive-coated area. Once the top is covered, spray the adhesive on the bottom of the cone and wrap the remaining area with moss. Assemble the tree by pressing the bottom of the cone onto the top of the trunk. Conceal the plaster with sheet moss. Place the tree in the terra-cotta pot. Decorate the tree as desired using a strand of wooden beads, securing the thread at intervals with straight pins, or use dried vine or French wired ribbon. Add miniature ornaments to continue the diminutive scale.

Noah's Ark Tree

Decorate tree with animal figures and tiny arks.

Christmas Fragrance

Hang homemade potpourri sachets from your tree to enhance the evergreen fragrance of your Christmas tree. Mix:

1 c. lavender flowers
8 c. dried rose petals
1 tbsp. ground cloves
4 drops rose oil

2 tbsp. each ground all spice, ground cinnamon, and ground orrisroot

Seal in an airtight container for six weeks before wrapping in pieces of meshed material secured with satin ribbons.

Grape Ornaments

Make bunches of grapes using tiny glass ornaments. Assemble about 25 glass balls of the same color, ranging in size from $5/8$ inch to 1 inch. Remove the wire hanger from one $5/8$-inch ball. Fold the tip of a pipe cleaner into a hook and poke it into the opening, so that it catches inside the ball and holds it securely. String the remaining balls on the pipe cleaner by their wire hangers, increasing the size as you go. Make a tendril by coiling another piece of pipe cleaner around a nail. Twist the tendril, together with a fabric leaf, to pipe-cleaner stem to finish the cluster.

Christmas Tree Prayer

This year, Lord, may our Christmas tree remind us
that our life in You will never die.
As we gather 'round its lights and bright decorations,
remind us to speak only words of love,
in honor of You, the Prince of Love,
whose birth we celebrate.

Amen.